The Mystery of Love

Also available from HarperCollins by the same author

The Gaze of Love

SISTER WENDY BECKETT

The Mystery of Love

Saints in art through the centuries

HarperCollins*Publishers*

for my friends, Annie and Peter Frankel

HarperCollins*Religious*
Part of HarperCollins*Publishers*
77-85 Fulham Palace Road, London W6 8JB

First published in Great Britain
in 1996 by HarperCollins*Religious*

1 3 5 7 9 10 8 6 4 2

These meditations were originally published
in the UK in the *Catholic Herald* as part of
Sister Wendy Beckett's regular series of
meditations on art. The publishers wish to thank
the publishers and staff of the *Catholic Herald*
for their kind co-operation.

A catalogue record for this book
is available from the British Library

ISBN 0 551 03012–7

Printed and bound in Great Britain by
Caledonian International Book Manufacturing Ltd, Glasgow

Extracts from 'Simple Prayer,' *The Clergy Review*,
February 1978 by Wendy Mary Beckett
reproduced with permission.

contents

v

Part Two – Images of Love

introduction

When I was young, I longed to be a saint: what was I longing for? I think it was for certainty that my life had been, in the most profound sense, a 'success', that great glorious success that is sanctity. We revere the saints, we imitate them, theirs is the only true and lasting glory. Very clearly, this desire is, unconsciously, as worldly as that of the writer who wants to write a masterpiece or the politician who yearns to be Prime Minister or President. None of these ambitions has the least to do with what Jesus preached – that lowliness, that love for last place, that readiness to die and be forgotten. Jesus never countenanced anything at all that boosted the ego. If saints want to 'sit on his right hand and his left in the Kingdom', then his answer is an uncompromising 'No'. To be concerned with oneself in any way, to watch one's growth in 'holiness' or 'prayer', to be spiritually ambitious: all this Jesus earnestly sets his face against. He tells us that the one sole virtue is obedience: 'I do always the things that please him', he says of his Father.

Obedience is the most demanding of all the virtues, because it never allows us a safe ride, a casual following of the rule. No, obedience means always looking at God and making our decisions in response to what we see is 'the mind of Christ'. His mind is all and only love, but that, too, is no easy answer. Love is an emotional word and in the Christian context is best translated as 'respect', or the biblical 'honour'. To honour others, to respect them, means to put their interests and rights before or at least, equal with, our own. It subdues the ego before the needs of our neighbour, it leads us to listen to what others say and demand, to balance well what is best for them (in our poor judgement, but the only judgement we have). This concentrated respectfulness is obedience to the Father – and it is the way Jesus summons us to live.

There is no space in such a life for ambition, however noble. St Paul, as so often, sums it up when he speaks of Jesus having 'become our holiness'. It is worth pondering this and the implications. If Jesus is our holiness, then we have sacrificed a holiness that is our own, self-achieved and self-comforting. It is extremely painful to live without any inner affirmation that one is pleasing to God, though our examinations of conscience may reassure us that we are not deliberately pursuing any act or attitude that we know to be unloving. But who can prove real purity of motive? Or who can assess what lies behind outward goodness? Having Jesus as our holiness means a total act of trust that, if something is to be done or changed, it will be made clear to us. Meanwhile, we set our sights on him, and surrender. Surrender is another word for obedience – that constant looking towards the Spirit with the urgent prayer to be enabled to receive the grace to give what he asks. When our total gaze is upon the Father, when our total prayer is for the grace of the Spirit, when we are totally receptive to the 'Yes' that St Paul says is 'always in Jesus', then we will have become saints. But we shall not know it. The self-regard that would see our sanctity is the great disqualifier. In practical terms, holiness is for other people, to be delighted in, imitated, revered. It is not our own concern, but God's. What is our part in this? Quite simply it is to pray.

The essential act of prayer is to stand unprotected before God. What will God do? He will take possession of us. That he should do this is the whole purpose of life. We know we belong to God; we know, too, if we are honest, that almost despite ourselves, we keep a deathly hold on our own autonomy. We are willing, in fact, very ready to pay God lip service (just as we are ready to talk prayer rather than to pray), because waving God as a banner keeps our conscience quiet. But really to belong to God is another matter. It means having nothing left for ourselves, always bound to the will of Another, no sense of interior success to comfort us, living in the painful acknowledgement of being 'unprofitable servants'. It is a terrible thing to be a fallen creature, and for most of the time we busily push this truth out of our awareness. But prayer places us helpless before God, and we taste the full bitterness of what we are. 'Our God is a consuming fire', and my filth crackles as he seizes hold of me; he 'is all light' and my darkness shrivels under his blaze. It is this naked blaze of God that makes prayer so terrible. For most of the time, we can persuade ourselves we are good enough, good as the next man, perhaps even better, who knows? Then we come to prayer – real prayer, unprotected prayer – and there is nothing left in us, no grounds on which to stand.

Normally, as we grow older, we become progressively skilled in coping with life. In most departments, we acquire techniques that we can fall back on when interest and attention wilt. It is part of maturity that there is always some reserve we can tap. But this is not so in prayer. It is the only human activity that depends totally and solely on its intrinsic truth. We are there before God – or rather, to the degree that we are there before God – we are exposed to all that he is, and he can neither deceive nor be deceived. It is not that we want to deceive, whether God or anybody else, but with other people, we cannot help our human condition of obscurity. We are not wholly there for them, nor they for us. We are simply not able to be so. Nor should we be: no human occasion calls for our total presence, even were it within our power to offer it. But prayer calls for it. Prayer is prayer if we want it to be. Ask yourself: What do I really want when I pray? Do you want to be possessed by God? Or, to put the same question more honestly, do you want to want it? Then you have it. The one point Jesus stressed and repeated and brought up again is that: 'Whatever you ask the Father, he will grant it to you'. His insistence on faith and perseverance are surely other ways of saying the same thing: you must really want, it must engross you. 'Wants' that are passing, faint emotional desires that you do not press with burning conviction, these are things you do not ask 'in Jesus' name; how could you? But what you really want, 'with all your heart and soul and mind and strength', that Jesus pledges himself to see that you are granted. He is not talking only, probably not even primarily, of 'prayer of petition', but of prayer. When you set yourself down to pray, WHAT DO YOU WANT? If you want God to take possession of you, then you are praying. That is all prayer is. There are no secrets, no shortcuts, no methods. Prayer is the utterly ruthless test of your sincerity. It is the one place in all the world where there is nowhere to hide. That is its utter bliss – and its torment.

Bliss or no, it is terrible to live with, to face up to its simplicity. I long to tell myself that the reason why 'I can't pray' is that I've never been taught, the right books have passed me by, the holy guru never came down my street. Hence the eager interest in books and articles on prayer – all obscuring from me my lack of true desire. Hence the enthusiasm for the holy retreat-givers, the directors, who will serve me as irrefutable alibi. If there were more to do, would I not do it? (I fast twice a week, I give tithes of all I possess . . .) No, I would not do it, I have no intention of doing it, but of course, to admit this to myself would rack me with guilt. Remember the rich young man? He had all the right words. 'Good Master, what must I do?' And Jesus tried to jolt him into reality. Why use words like 'good' when you do not understand them? But he persisted, and Jesus gave him what the young man truly believed he was asking for: Jesus tells him 'what to do', and of course, he goes away sorrowful, because Jesus has taken it out of the region of ideals and emotions and rendered his Father's claims in plain fact. 'Sell, give, come follow me.' It was not what was wanted. Do you think this man went away conscious of his inner falsehood and realizing that he was quite unprepared to look at God straight? I hope he did, but I fear he may well have been sad because the Master's claims 'could not' be met, that he barricaded himself down behind the excuse of 'inability', which he convinced himself he longed to be able to overcome.

If you desire to stand surrendered before God, then you are standing there; it needs absolutely nothing else. Prayer is the last thing we should feel discouraged about. It concerns nobody except God – always longing only to give himself to us in love – and my own decision. And that too is God's, 'who works in us to will and to effect'. In a very true sense, there is nothing more to say about prayer – 'the simplest thing out'. However, two practical comments. The first is that prayer must have time. It is part of our normal living, the heart of it, and it can't fit in along with or during other activities, any more than sleep can. Of itself, it must swamp whatever we try to combine with it. It demands the whole of you, to hold you in the consuming Fire, and then you can go about the rest of the day still ablaze with him. There is a tendency today for people to say, with greater or less distress, that they have no time for prayer. This is not true.

(Forgive me). What they mean is, they have not got a peaceful hour or two peaceful half-hours or even three peaceful twenty minutes. If that is the day God has given them, then he awaits their praying hearts under precisely these conditions. They are testing conditions, surely, but never impossible. Nobody goes through a day without here and there the odd patch, a five minute break, a ten minute pause. If you do truly want to pray, well then, pray. Take these times, poor crumbs of minutes though they be, and give yourself to God in them. You will not be able to feel prayerful in them, but that is beside the point. You pray for God's sake, you are there for him to look on you, to love you, to take his holy pleasure in you. What can it matter whether you feel any of this or get any comfort from it? We should be misers in prayer, scraping up these flinders of time and holding them out trustfully to the Father. But we should also watch out for the longer stretches which we may be missing because we don't want to see them. Many things that are pleasant and profitable, TV programmes, books, conversations, may have at times to be sacrificed. But you will make this and any other sacrifice if you hunger and thirst for God to possess you, and this is my whole point. There is time enough for what matters supremely to us, and there always will be. The exact amount of time is up to our common sense. For most people, an hour would be a norm, remembering constantly that I am talking simply about being there: the quality is a question for God. Tired or out of sorts, I am still equally myself for him to take hold of me. I will feel nothing of it, that's all.

The other practical point is: what shall I do during prayer? (How eagerly people long to be told the answer! For that would make me safe against God, well protected: I would know what to do!) But the answer is of the usual appalling simplicity: stand before God unprotected, and you will know yourself what to do. I mean this in utter earnest. Methods are of value, naturally, but only as something to do 'if I want to', which in this context of response to God means: if he wants me to. I may feel drawn to meditate, to sing to him, to stay before him in, say, an attitude of contrition or praise; most often I shall probably want to do nothing but be in his presence. Whether I am aware of that presence does not matter. I know he is there, whatever my feelings, just as Jesus knew when he felt abandoned on the cross. What pure praise of the Father's love; to feel abandoned and yet stay content before him, saying: 'Father, into your hands . . .' We cannot sufficiently emphasize to ourselves that prayer is God's concern, and his one desire is 'to come and make his abode with us'. Do we believe him or not? Of course, I can cheat. If I choose not to be there for him, and since I am not yet transformed into Jesus, to some extent I always do protect myself against the impact of his love, then that is cause for grief. But it is creative grief. It drives us helpless to Jesus to be healed. We say to him: 'If you want to, you can make me clean'. But he answers: 'I do want to – but do you?' That 'wanting' is ever the crux of the matter.

Is there any way of telling whether we do want Jesus to surrender us to his Father? In *Gaudy Night* Dorothy Sayers has one character ask another when we can know which are our overmastering desires? And she is told: When they have overmastered us. This is a very wise comment. If God has taken you so deeply into his love that he has transformed you into Jesus, then you have indeed wanted him with overmastering passion. But if this has not yet happened – even if, humbly, you must say that nothing much at all has happened ('This man went home justified rather than the other'), it can only be because, secretly, deep down you have not wanted it to happen. This is something you cannot help – these hidden desires that shape our course are beyond our control. But they are not beyond God's control. His whole reason for giving us the sacraments is to open up these recesses to grace and change what we think we want into actuality. Our actions show us what we do in fact want – depressing sight, and sadly coexistent with an emotional consciousness of wholly other wants. We have to hand this over to God, both explicitly, and by immersing our poverty in the strong objective prayer of the eucharist and the sacraments. There we have Jesus giving himself totally to the Father and taking us with him. Then we can almost see, acted out before us, what the Spirit is trying to effect in our own depths. Let him effect it – let him be God for us. Whatever the past or my fears of the future, here and now, O Holy Spirit, utter within me the total Yes of Jesus to the Father.

I have not dwelt in this book on the lives of personalities of the saints, partly because we know little about most of them, and partly because what really interests me is their attitude, their love. This is constant, the essence of all and any holiness. It is our greatest joy to know that, however poorly we love God, there have been and are others who have understood the lonely call of Jesus. They have accepted to hang without support in the terrible nothingness of 'no holiness of their own', no comforting inner feedback. They have agreed to be the last, to fall into the ground and die, to take up the cross, to wash the feet of others.

May we learn to give Jesus utter freedom within us, so that everything we are and do may be used for the mystery of love.

Part One

Saints in Art

Duccio

The Calling of the Apostles Peter and Andrew, 1308–11

A twofold calling

It is somehow typical of St Andrew that he is depicted with his more famous brother, St Peter. We tend to think of St Peter as the elder, but perhaps he was merely the more forceful. It is a lovely touch in the gospels that it is not St Peter, the dynamic, the natural leader, who first finds Jesus, but the quieter and less noticeable St Andrew.

He spent the day with Jesus, watching him, and then went home to tell his brother that 'we have found the Messiah'. In other words, St Andrew 'found' Jesus because he contemplated him, he spent time 'seeing'. Duccio's great picture suggests this shade of difference between the brothers.

St Peter is turned to Jesus in a stance of authoritative attention. He is tense, active, ready to spring into obedience. But St Andrew looks pensive, not exactly hesitant, but deliberating, weighing up the meaning of this summons and its consequences. His is a praying face, one that lives in the peace of reflection, as opposed to Peter's instinctive activity. But both hold the net.

In the calling to become fishers of men, to found the Church, to be its priests, both attitudes are necessary: there must always be the two sides of love, prayer and action. Prayer is less prominent, as is only expected, since the movements of the heart are essentially secret, but no work for God can be done without it.

In a way, Duccio shows the two Apostles as twins, a single apostolate with two dimensions, as if to hint at this twofold attitude in any saint. We – incipient saints – are in exactly the same position as the fighting brothers; Jesus cuts across all our neat divisions of the ordinary and the religious.

He calls out to us wherever we are and at any time. We only hear this call if, like St Andrew, we have spent time with him in quiet, letting the truth of Jesus imprint itself in our being. Then once we have heard, we need to look again at him for the strength to respond. If we pray, we shall live in obedience to the Father: if we live in obedience, we shall be drawn all the more to prayer.

The active and contemplative lives are functions of each other: they can never be wholly apart, even if the emphasis must differ for each separate vocation. St Andrew, fortunate man, was given 'the better part', with its hiddenness but also its weighty responsibilities. He, as much as St Peter, is the rock on which the Church is founded.

Rogier van der Weyden

Magdalen Reading, c.1435

Fragment of forgiveness

Rogier van der Weyden has an emotional power, a spiritual beauty, that makes him even more moving than his great contemporary, Jan van Eyck. One of the tragedies of non survival, of the vulnerability of a work of art, is that this wonderful picture of the Magdalen is only a fragment: we can never visualize what has been destroyed, only lament it. But there is an ironic appropriateness in this sad mutilation.

Mary Magdalen is a saint whom we can only see in fragmentary glimpses. We know that this reading woman is the Magdalen because she has by her side the alabaster vase with which Christ's feet were anointed at the supper with Simon. Yet there is no evidence that this anointing woman, of bad local repute, was the same woman as the sister of Martha, who sat silent at the feet of Jesus when he visited their house, or with the Mary Magdalen out of whom 'seven devils' were cast and who met the Risen Jesus in the garden.

So we have only a picture of this saint cobbled together from the gospel jigsaw, and maybe incorrectly. If she was indeed a sinner, here we see her in the quiet watchfulness of prayer.

She sits on the ground, always a symbol of humility. Unless we accept, with contentment, our unimportance, we cannot receive the Lord in truth. Self-centred prayer, aware of self, depending upon its own emotional reactions, interested in how it 'feels', depending upon the controlling power of the ego: such prayer is not that of Jesus.

Standing upon our own two feet is a mark of independence, while prayer needs the full and loving admission that we are totally dependent.

We sit upon the earth of our reality. We surrender. But we do not sit passive, inert, slothful. We do what God asks of us, even if we can never know what that is. We seek only to respond, never to initiate. Magdalen, unaware of her own beauty, holds the holy book reverently, delicately.

Her face is wholly at peace, as she listens. She is not ravaged by the emotion of repentance, self-indulgence, and she dresses modestly but elegantly. There is no parade, no ostentatious piety. Perhaps significantly, in prayer she reveals her underskirt, hidden in normal occupations: it is pure gold. But her exposure is to Jesus, and to him alone.

Lorenzo Lotto

Holy Family with St Anne, 1535

The intimacy of an outsider

Although it is Anne who gets a separate mention in the title, it is St Joseph who gives this painting its special poignancy. Lotto is a peculiarly sensitive artist, always alert to nuances that may pass others by, and it is quite in character that he should be fascinated by St Joseph.

This saint has a strange ambivalence of role: head of the Holy Family and yet its least significant member; supporter of Mary and Jesus in one sense, yet supported by them in another. We know practically nothing about him. St Matthew tells us what was said (or revealed) to him, but we never hear his word, only his thoughts and their consequences. He is a shadowy figure in the first chapters of Matthew and Luke, and then he silently disappears: pious imagination is left to provide him with a personality.

This cannot be by chance. St Joseph has always appealed to those who value the hidden life, the silent role of servant to others, a vocation to 'labour, suffer and be silent'.

But the middle verb is a vital one: this is an extremely difficult vocation. Many are forced into it by the circumstances of their lives, but it only becomes vocation, a way to holiness, if the suffering is taken sweetly and wisely, without the dramatics of self-pity or the bitterness of frustration. Lotto shows us a loving circle: Mary. Jesus – and St Anne. These three are tight-knit, a closed unit. They look out and across at St Joseph, who is not in their corner, not one of the intimates. He is well aware of this exclusion: few gazes are more touching than that exchanged between the young wife sad for her excluded husband, wishful to admit him to the charmed circle but conscious of his outer position, and the elderly saint. Joseph yearns across to the threesome, his head beneath the open window, symbol of his role as man and worker.

He is the one who must leave the safety of the family to earn their bread, the one whose task demands that he be absent for much of the day from the loving presence of his family. Joseph appears here as the outsider, but through vocation not choice. His peaceful hands show that he enters upon his humble role with gentle dignity.

The love that consumes him is not to find expression in long periods of intimacy with his beloved, but in doing what best serves their needs. He puts God first, and himself nowhere, but it costs. It is a low-key but totally redemptive death-to-self.

Luca Giordano

St Michael the Archangel, c.1663

Luca Giordano was nicknamed 'Luca fa presto' – do-it-quick Luke, because of his dazzling speed of execution. It seems rather an appropriate trait for one who dares paint an angel, creatures of air and fire that are all spirit. St Michael, whose name translates as 'who is as God', is a living symbol of divine energy, and is usually shown in art as he is here: battling triumphantly with the spirit of evil.

Giordano has imagined a particularly repulsive devil, compounded of grossness and fury. He straddles the width of the picture, amidst a whirl of demonic limbs: this is the great expulsion, when Michael cast out from God's presence all who refused to serve their Lord.

Michael himself is radiantly fair, barely held within the confines of the picture as he plunges a long diagonal of mortal rejection into the devilish body.

The archangel is totally dominant, totally assured and calm, totally beautiful. In the context of this painting, it is difficult to remember that evil never has been overcome once and for all, and that the battle Giordano depicts takes place incessantly. It is always a temptation, the wish that all nay-saying to God's love could be utterly destroyed in the world. But it is in our own personal world, our own spirit, that the battle takes place, and there will never be a settled finish. We know the outcome: it will be the triumph of goodness, just as Giordano shows it, but the battle may last throughout our life.

The 'devil' is within: he represents everything in our hearts that does not want God. A holy Jesuit once said: there is part of me that wants no part of Jesus: a terrifying reflection.

Consciously we would all disown it, but our actual conduct tells us whether it is true or not. Is everything in us given to God? Or are there areas that we keep from his Love, our 'own' places, in which we can do as we please, forge – everything but our desires? That strong will to self is what Michael is attacking: the archangel is as much part of us as the dark angel. Michael is the divine Power that Our Lord freely gives us, in the sacraments and in the prayer that activates that sacramental grace.

When we look at Jesus, we allow him to fight for us against ourselves, to be our St Michael against our devil. Jesus will always conquer: but we must give him space. Prayer is this space, this act of effective trust. It is not we who battle but God within us, and so we can rejoice already in the victory.

Lorenzo Lotto

St Catherine of Alexandria, 1522

Serenity based on faith

Lorenzo Lotto is an artist who always sees beneath the surface, and he found St Catherine of Alexandria a fascinating subject.

Martyr saints are fairly common in art, but scholar saints are not – let alone a female scholar. Legend places St Catherine in Alexandria, that famously intellectual city, with none so learned as the youthful Catherine. But hers was a Christian learning, and it brought her a martyr's death. She was condemned to be killed on a spiked wheel (hence the 'Catherine wheel' of firework fame), but it shattered at her touch and she was eventually beheaded.

This giant wheel is her attribute in art, and Lotto, with typical subtlety, has wrapped it in a field of her silken cloak. She leans on it, insouciantly, a ferocious engine tamed and domesticated. One forlorn spike sticks uselessly out on either side. The saint's expression is ambiguous, as so often in a Lotto portrait.

One slender aristocratic hand displays her ring: she is betrothed to Christ and has no attention for any earthly lover. The other hand plays negligently with the long sweep of her martyr's palm. As a patrician, she is nobly pearled, and as a bride of Christ the King, she is crowned.

Sumptuously clad, against a background of rich brocade, St Catherine tilts her charming head and looks at us. She has a face of pink-and-white perfection, a clever face with an ironic curl of her mouth. She seems both sweet and strong, completely in command of herself.

Yet this is the girl who will be torn apart by life, hounded to a very messy grave. All her gifts of mind and body are to be taken from her with a vicious cruelty, and she will have no power whatsoever. To Lotto, this material power is unimportant. Catherine may be killed but she cannot be destroyed. Whatever is done to her, she remains and will remain herself.

He shows us a profundity of detachment, of inner serenity, based, we feel, not on her extraordinary personality but on her faith. She is secure in God: in a true sense, no one can touch her. Living in the faith means utter safety. 'Though he slay me, yet will I trust in Him.'

St Catherine half-smiles as she leans upon her terrible wheel and distances herself from material harm. The presence of prayer protects her, that prayer which is our awareness of God. Knowing of his love, the saint can afford to relax amidst trials and torture, and so can we.

Giotto

St Francis Preaching to the Birds

Winged sermons

St Francis of Assisi is the one saint everybody loves, and his affection for the natural world is part of that universal attraction. We are charmed that he should communicate with the birds and that these wild creatures should be aware of God's message through him. In fact, being able to talk to birds is a common human desire, and we are glad to see it being realized in another.

Yet Giotto shows us infinitely more than a fable to charm us. For all its sweetness, this is a sober picture, with its solid human forms and tall and realistic tree, while between them the birds form docile ranks. Francis, as so often, has a witness, a friar, less ethereal in form and wholly astonished at what he sees. The witness is the reassurance that the event is 'true' just as the tree serves to set it in a real world and not in romantic fantasy.

But it is only a partially real world. The background of gold distances the sermon from its earthly setting. The discourse between man and animal takes place partly on the soil of earth, partly in the radiance of heaven. St Francis is unsmiling, and he is addressing his avian congregation with intense seriousness.

What is too easily forgotten is the motive for this sermon. Francis is preaching to the fowls of the air because he cannot make himself heard by the men and women of his time. He is acting out a parable: how is it, the legend asks, that even the irrational creation can sense the demands of God while the rational refuses even to listen? The birds, wildest and least disciplined of natural beings, form obedient and attentive lines before the saint. They may not understand, but they are conscious of a holy presence.

But we do understand, or at least, can understand if we want to. Not to listen, not to learn from him, is a terrible rejection of God.

This picture, seemingly so quaintly delightful, is a summons to listen. Whether we listen to the Holy Spirit within or to his voice in others 'blessed are those that hear the Word and do it'.

Raphael

St George and the Dragon, 1506

A symbolic hero

St George has the distinction of having been with us, in one form or another, from the earliest Pre-Christian ages.

Humankind have always needed a hero who fights for them against the evil one, whether he is the Green Man, attacking winter, or the mythical Warrior, attacking the enemy, (Beowulf, Samson or Perseus) or St George attacking the dragon. The dragon is all that destroys us, and this is far more than the external foe.

We respond immediately and profoundly to this image because we are all, if we are honest with ourselves, aware of the struggle within against the tyranny of the ego. St Paul famously lamented that he desired the good but did not do it, hated the evil but did do it.

As Our Lord said more succinctly: the spirit indeed is willing but the flesh is weak. St George is the spirit, seated on the white steed of grace, armoured by the power of the God who can do all things, and bearing the lance of a pure intention. The dragon is the flesh, greedy and violent, responsive only to its own desires, devourer of innocence.

Raphael's dragon is a good one, fierce and supple, no easy victim for the saint's lance. St George, though, is resolutely unperturbed, serene in the total security of his armour. Since he is by definition relying on the power of God, and refusing to look to his own power for any support, it stands to reason that he has no cause for anxiety.

Even the little princess, waiting like other virgins before her to be dragon-fodder, prays with a sweet serenity. She is the contemplative complement to St George's martial activity, the bride that will be his lifelong partner when the battle is over.

Realistically, that battle will only end with death, so in a sense she is the symbol of our heaven. Raphael has set her in a supremely ordered landscape, a still contrast to the windblown foreground, with its sinister unbalance of a cave from which the dragon emerges to ravish. The picture does not disguise the labour and care needed to slay our dragon: St George is wholly intent, but it also makes clear how triumphantly we can fight when it is God who is our protector. The essential meaning of this story is one of immense hope.

Girolamo da Cremona

detail from Frontispiece:
Aristotle 'Opera', 1483

Human knowledge is not enough

A copy of the works of Aristotle made in Venice in 1483 was illustrated by Girolamo da Cremona. Here is a detail from the painting that introduces his First Book of Metaphysics, and it shows a row of philosophers.

That must be Aristotle in the middle, holding forth to three generic Greek philosophers, all marked by their meditative stance, with hats pulled low over the brow to avert distractions, as is Aristotle's own hat. But his three Greek friends also keep their hands and arms resolutely shielded: their task is mental, not physical.

Aristotle, to show his perfect balance, can both think and act. On his left are two Jewish philosophers: Solomon crowned and the anonymous author of the Book of Wisdom, or some other biblical thinker. The surprises come at either end: St Thomas – who gladly acknowledged his debt to Aristotle, and an ape. St Thomas is the only one to eschew bright colours. He does not need them: his brightness is Jesus and not his own. The ape is the only one not attending to the preachers, and that is the point of da Cremona's painting: to be human means to desire understanding. The ape seems to be eating, a sign of preferring the material and experimental to the ascetic journeyings of thought. The closest animal to man, by medieval reckoning, yet the monkey cannot share our most fundamental trait: that we are not only able to know but cannot live a fulfilled life without knowledge. But it is a difficult concept.

We so easily use our knowledge as a means of control, and while it is precisely that 'physically', it can never be that 'metaphysically'. God is the totality of mystery. The intentness of the six philosophers has a certain sadness. What they most desire – to understand God – is absolutely beyond them. Only St Thomas, clutching his Bible and using it – whereas Solomon's closed book can only be the Old Testament – looks at peace. All prayer, all contact with God, demands of us this profound sacrifice: we must surrender to unknowing. This surrender goes very deep, cutting away at our very nature. We survive, we grow, we mature, through the wise use of our minds. Without thought, all worlds are closed to us except the small one of our ego – and even that we cannot comprehend. But we are called by Jesus to 'know the Truth' and let it 'set us free', while all the time accepting that he is 'the Truth' and we are set free into his life, not into a control of our own. At Thomas's feet lies the Cross; at the pagans' lies the sword. We must live by one or the other.

16

Raphael

An Allegory, (Vision of a Knight), c.1504

The sword and the flower

Raphael was a pupil of Perugino, and his earliest work has all the characteristics of his teacher: small round faces, gracious forms, an air of sweet ethereality.

An Allegory shows a young knight dreaming between two young women, one stern and brandishing a sword, the other the detail here reproduced. The meaning is usually taken to be that the youth must choose between virtue – the austere brunette – and pleasure – the gentle blonde – sometimes divinised into the goddess of wisdom, Minerva, and the goddess of love, Venus.

But it is difficult to think of this modest girl as in any way a temptation. She stands shyly to one side, offering a delicate spray of blossom, and it seems to me that she is almost certainly prayer, the contemplative life, just as her 'rival' is work, the apostolic life. The Christian warrior can choose either as his vocation, though of course, we all find that we are naturally drawn to one or the other.

Prayer is wreathed with what looks like rosary beads, which one hand is telling, and she offers no external proofs of virtue. All she has to show is a useless flower. We remember that Jesus told overactive Martha that Mary, sitting 'uselessly' at his feet, had chosen 'the best part'. The personification of prayer is still, peaceful, intent upon offering her small spray of blossom. She takes no notice of the world behind her, and her eyes are downcast, looking within, not at the sleeping youth.

This is the contemplative repose that we all need, and it is probably true to say that the 'choice' before the knight is to choose both. Although some are definitely called to a life of enclosed prayer, and others to a life of missionary activity, each of these extremes includes the other.

We cannot work for God unless we are kept alive by prayer: we cannot pray unless we are selflessly aware of the world's needs, (not specifically but as sharing responsibility). Prayer sweetens the world's atmosphere, so that the apostolate can breathe.

Most people are called to live within these two extreme parameters, praying and serving God while living a normal life in the marketplace and at home. Perhaps the allegory says: do not forget that you have two weapons, a sword and a flower, and you need them both.

18

Eustache le Sueur

The Annunciation, c.1650

God's messenger within

Of all the mysteries of the faith, the Annunciation is the most lovingly and frequently portrayed. There is hardly an Old Master who has not tried to wrestle with this sacred drama, this quintessential confrontation, when heaven meets earth, and human history changes radically and for ever. Being human ourselves, we identify more with Mary, trembling or awed or contemplative, according to the artists own vision.

Le Sueur sees Mary as almost unaware of her holy visitor, too lost in prayer to do more than sink more deeply still into the silence of her total Yes to God. Perhaps he is suggesting that she did, in fact, 'see' nothing, that the encounter was an interior one, and that the angelic question was put to her wordlessly?

His Gabriel is exceptionally unearthly. Many artists show him standing or kneeling: Le Sueur has him floating, indifferent to the ground, wafted into Mary's chamber by the breath of the Spirit and on the point of dissolving into pure light.

He billows luminously in the sunlit air, garments aflutter and alight with changing colour. His hair streams in the heavenly wind and he seems less substantial than the tall stalk of lilies that symbolize Mary's state of immaculate grace. Yet the name Gabriel means: God is my strength. A name of immense power. The power is not in the angel, it is God's power, transmitted through him.

When God sends a messenger, (an angel) the message does not come externally. It brings with it the potential for its answer, internally, so that 'How can this be?' is always answered from within. If God asks something, it is absolutely certain that he himself will make it possible. When it is our decision, to give something to God, to offer him a sacrifice, however virtuous, then we can only count on human strength. But when it is he who asks, then the strength comes with the asking. We are never called to initiate with God, only to respond. His messenger, his Gabriel, will speak to us from the context of our actual lives with all their elements, both material and spiritual.

Our present situation, examined in prayer, will always reveal what is being asked of us. Like Mary, we are receiving a summons, but not in outward forms. Le Sueur shows beautifully the inwardness of the mystery, and its force. Gabriel is an empowerment, blessing and making possible. Mary 'heard' him because she sought God with all her energies. May we also 'hear'.

Bartolomé Murillo

The Infant St John with a Lamb, 1660-5

Sentimental or striking?

Murillo, once considered the greatest artist of the seventeenth century, is today out of favour. What our ancestors thought heavenly in its spirituality, we regard as sentimental. Not many people may take to this little St John embracing his lamb.

Yet it is striking as a painting, with the dull brightness of the overcast sky above and the misty autumnal browns of the trees and grasslands on either side. If we can forget about our dislike for gleaming curls on a small boy and the child's sheer prettiness, we can perhaps recover the meaning that inspired Murillo himself and his first viewers. He shows us a lonely child, uncared for, barefoot upon the rocks, ill-clad against the winds. But John is absorbed in his relationship with a lamb, the Lamb: his symbolic Lord.

Murillo does not spell out whether we are to take the lamb as literally Jesus, consoling his prophet before the time, or whether John is imagined as embracing the Lord in symbol, rather as another might kiss a crucifix, but the literal facts are unimportant.

What he is trying to show us is the depth of the child's affection for the Lamb of God. Jesus, the Lamb, returns the embrace, brushing softly against the child's cheek, laying a thin leg on the child's arm.

Because Murillo is a technician of genius, all the textures are palpable, and only prejudice holds us back from awareness of their feel. But to what end? The end is to arouse our devotion, to depict, in parable, the tenderness and immediacy of divine love. It can be responded to at any age and in any form. Murillo may even include the suggestion that a child caressing a beloved animal is experiencing one of the myriad forms of the love of God. All love, says this painting, is sacred, a means of touching God and being touched by him. Grace comes from all directions and often unexpectedly. If cruelty is the essential sin, then reverence is the essential virtue.

It can be called 'love' but the word is ambiguous. It should be seen as reverence, a happy readiness always to respect, to be generous and non-judgemental, to hug even a lowly beast, never to close one's heart: this is what holiness is all about. It is the only goal of human existence.

Georges de la Tour

St Sebastian and Irene

Light and shadow

De la Tour is a painter of such haunting beauty that it seems incredible that, like Vermeer, he was forgotten for centuries. Interestingly, both these artists are fascinated, held entranced, by the mystery of light, and it may be that it has taken the invention of electricity, with its harsh brilliance, to open our eyes more sensitively to the wonder of the sun and of flame.

Here de la Tour depicts the famous legendary scene in which St Irene grieves over the nearly lifeless body of St Sebastian and begins the long work of nursing him back to health. Men from his regiment had been ordered to use him for target practice, since he refused to worship the Roman Emperor as divine, an obligation laid upon all soldiers in the imperial army.

Artists usually show his body riddled with arrow wounds, but de la Tour, deliberately non-dramatic, has only one shaft piercing him in the breast. Sebastian is hidden in the shadows, an anonymous body which has aroused Irene's compassion. We are, of course, reminded of the Passion of Christ, which the martyrs re-enact, and where the Body of Jesus, taken down from the cross, is surrounded by his mother and the holy women.

But in the Deposition scene, it is always easy to identify the mourners: here, there is a problem which is St Irene, and which is her daughter and maidservants? Is she the kneeling figure, richly dressed, so tenderly intent upon her patient? Or is she the central standing figure, older and more beautiful, hands held out in astonished pity?

Two other women flank her, one almost obliterated by the darkness. The light plays tricks too. At first we may think the source of illumination is held by the kneeling girl, that it is a lantern or torch, and it may be, but the shape is puzzling, as is the way certain details are brightly lit, others obscured.

Perhaps this is all part of the sacred meaning. Light is the symbol of God: we cannot understand or control it, any more than we can tell, by looking, who is a 'saint' or who not. The event is one of loving compassion, of the desire to heal, of selflessness. If Sebastian was ready to die for Christ, Irene is ready to lie for him, to take risks, to give new time and care.

One saint is obvious, the other hidden. Does it matter? It is God, Light Itself, who knows and is active. We lower our intellectual pride and leave judgement to him.

24

Lorin de Chartres (studio of) Alsation School

St Timothy with the Martyrs' Palm

The light that is God

Stained glass is perhaps the perfect medium for religious art. Of its very nature, it is translucent, wholly receptive of the light, that profound image of God.

The saints are essentially those among us who have allowed the light to shine through them, keeping nothing secretly for themselves. (As a further bonus, we rarely know the names and biographies of stained-glass artists, so can delight in their work without the distractions of personal details).

This St Timothy is rather a remote figure, not wholly the dear surrogate son that he was to St Paul. That historical Timothy, as found in the Acts of the Apostles and St Paul's letters, was of course fairly austere: St Paul had to urge him to take a little wine 'for his health's sake', a young man weak in body, then, though obviously strong in spirit. What makes this window so powerful is the intensity of the form. St Timothy rises heavenward in one firm sweep. His body is tense with resolve, undeviatingly concentrated, which is the great sign of holiness.

The saint wants God so passionately that all else is subsumed in that one great desire. There are other things, perhaps many, but these do not exist of themselves: they are used and valued to the extent that they lead to God.

St Timothy holds one hand open and facing us. It is both a greeting and a blessing, and also a gesture of abnegation; it is only the empty hand that God can fill. It is a hand lifted to praise and to pray, a multi-purposed gesture.

The other hand is quite unambiguous: it holds a palm, symbol of the martyr. But the palm could also be read as a sword, the sword of the Spirit 'which is the word of God'.

The action of the hand may be simple, but the image that it holds admits complexity. Perhaps, like the other hand's gesture, the complexity is intentional, indicating that martyrdom and the work of preaching the Gospel are interchangeable? Central to the saint's forehead is a black mark, where a cobweb of lines meet.

Was there a fracture here? Or is this just an inept handling of the soldered supports that stained glass needs? It is, in any case, a *felix culpa*. The dark stain recalls to us that St Timothy is said to have been stoned to death, and it draws our gaze to his brow. It is in the mind, in the conscious and subconscious reality of our being, that we direct ourselves to the Lord.

The centre of a heart that truly loves is intense, unified, directed. May it be so with us.

Diego Velázquez

St John the Evangelist, c.1618

An unlikely medium

It was on the island of Patmos that St John had the vision which he recorded in the book of Revelations, otherwise known as the Apocalypse.

They were startling visions, still rather difficult to assimilate, but at least one image from them has become firmly enshrined in liturgical prayer. This was his vision of 'a woman, clothed with the sun', which corresponds with beautiful closeness to how we see the Virgin Mary. Velázquez painted this picture of St John (together with a companion picture of the Immaculate Conception) for the Carmelite Fathers, early and ardent advocates of the Immaculate Conception as a dogma of faith.

But Mary is very small and far away, a dimly gleaming presence. All our attention is fixed upon St John, an astonishing figure in his raw-boned realism. This John not only has no halo, but there are none of the conventional signs that mark him out as 'saint'. He is plain and youthful, his mouth over-full of teeth and his bare feet ungainly in their largeness.

At his left, very dim in the circumambient gloom, broods his eagle, the saint's emblem, chosen for him because of the rapturous flight of his writing: no evangelist is more spiritual, less earthly than John. Velázquez does not contradict this. His young saint is enraptured, transfixed by his heavenly visions: his expression is infinitely touching, almost incredulous with joy, almost rigid with the desire to describe faithfully what is vouchsafed to him.

But this ecstatic encounter is not granted to any ethereal figure. John is quite obviously an ordinary young man, somebody like ourselves. The symbolic eagle is tactfully in the background, and we are more conscious of the mystical because of its secular setting.

John comes across as lonely and poor, isolated on his small island and unprotected there. The tree behind him has an eerie awkwardness of form, the bark curling and protruding with almost Bosch-like effect. John seems to have nothing but his book of manuscripts and his pen: even ink is absent, as if to suggest that he is writing with the fluid of his spirit.

The bright and heavenly apparition is far away. Here on earth, John sits in darkness and alone, receiving the privilege of divine inspiration. This is how prayer works, the picture hints: God will reveal himself, but we must accept the conditions, his conditions, which will demand a readiness to look only at him and have him alone for our joy.

Andrea del Sarto

St Agnes

Calm in the face of martyrdom

Andrea del Sarto, with his lovely smudgy colour, shows St Agnes in a darkened landscape. Dawn is just breaking, catching the towers and strongholds of the city, from which she has been cast out.

There are no lasting human safeties for any of us, whether called to be martyrs or to die happily in our beds after a long lifetime. Essentially, we all sit outside the world's city, alone and looking upwards.

Agnes holds the palm, sign of her martyrdom. Christian piety had early equipped her with an attendant sheep: 'agnus', the lamb. It is a fitting sign for her youth and innocence and also for her holy vocation. Like the lamb of God, she too will be slain. She contemplates this fate without dismay: it is a very steady and peaceful gaze that she raises on high, and the soft morning light seems to presage the eternal dawning of the day, when the temporary night is left for ever and heavenly light shines eternal.

Del Sarto makes two things very clear. His young saint is extremely beautiful. Her garments may be simple, but they sweep around her in exquisite folds of tender primrose, green and pink. Yet, and this is del Sarto's second point, this lovely child waits in total faith for her life to be taken away from her. She is serious in her patience, well aware of the significance of death, holding herself ready, without any tension, to accept what is to come.

One hand holds the palm, the active hand, the human choice of God above self. The other hand, the inactive, rests quietly on the lamb, the mystic sign of God's presence. This is the contemplative hand, receiving, wordlessly, from the contact with her companion, the support of the true Lamb.

Jesus himself makes her state possible: she chooses, but it is he who makes that choice more wishful. It is an immensely peaceful picture, this steady waiting, alone in the semi-darkness, for God to do whatever he pleases. It sums up what it means to follow Christ.

Michelino da Besozzo

St Luke Painting the Virgin, c.1420

The danger of trivialization

St Luke seems always to have struck people as the most humanly attractive of the Evangelists, perhaps because the Acts of the Apostles enable him to flesh himself out a bit.

But legend has embroidered freely: he is said to have been not only a doctor but a painter, a close friend of Mary, the mother of Jesus, and the natural choice to paint her portrait. This story may seem innocent enough, but it dictates a great desire to domesticate the Scriptures, to recontextualize them, in a scenario of our comprehending.

Every great lady in medieval times had her portrait painted – so why not Mary? But turning Mary or the Apostles into contemporaries only obscures the reality of the Gospels. All the sweet intimate details are not meant for our knowing. Just as da Besozzo has turned Luke's symbolic ox into a delightful ox-type stag, so the unknowingness of Mary and Luke is diminished by a charming human image. We cannot afford human images, however appealing. Our calling is to encounter pure truth: 'Do not touch me, for I am not yet ascended', said Jesus, who has to go away in body before he can come to us in spirit.

God's instruments are never intended to be more than channels. The personalities of all who speak his Word must be subdued to the Word itself. Making prayers interesting, adding embellishments to our worship – in the way that this picture does to its central image – is a most subtle business and an ultimate test of our sincerity.

Do we want God, or 'our' God, made accessible, made easy? Yet of course we are right to use all the means to draw others to God, and to draw ourselves the same way. If anything works, we should use it. Ah, but what does it mean 'to work'? Might we not be deluding ourselves, substituting the human for the divine and erecting an alternative faith, that makes fewer demands and leaves us feeling good? Keeping the balance between what we need, frail as we are, and what we want, is only possible through Jesus.

We shall always cheat – even innocently – always paint small lovely pictures of Mary that disguise the loneliness of having so little contact with her. The great rough ox of God will always be trivialized into a pet ox that can sit on our floor and be part of our activity.

Luke is controlling Mary here, by painting her, and the artist is controlling Luke, and all that he stands for. To give up all control and let God be the only artist, whose work we shall never see here on earth: that is what our prayer achieves in us. By letting go now, in faith, we make it possible for God to overwhelm our fears and establish us in Jesus, the True One.

Giovanni Battista Cima da Conegliano

St Jerome in a Landscape, 1500-10

A penitent and prayerful saint

St Jerome has always had a great appeal for artists. He could be shown in his study: Jerome the scholar, translating the Scriptures and giving the Vulgate to the Church.

Again, he could be shown in the desert, Jerome the tempted, who fled the seductions of Rome and lived a life of extreme austerity, much afflicted by the evil spirits that harass a mind deprived of its proper nutriment.

The third image is the one that Cima gives us here: Jerome the penitent. The sins for which he did such ferocious penitence seem innocuous to use. He was, for example, much distressed by his love for Vergil and other Latin authors, and grieved that he had spent time on them that he should have reserved for prayer and bible study.

The specifics of his contrition may be unconvincing, but Cima shows us forcibly the need that a saint must feel to make reparation for all the continual and unnoticed ways in which God is not loved enough.

He shows us Jerome about to beat his breast with a stone, an emphatic *mea culpa*. He is bathed in sunlight, but an abyss separates him from the cheerful secular world that goes about its business in the middle distance. He does not live among its green plains and blue rivers, with friend and activities, but alone on a craggy height, with a vulture to remind him of his mortality and his attendant lion to remind him of his fleshliness.

Legend has it that Jerome fearlessly removed a thorn from the lion's foot and thereafter enjoyed his protective comradeship. It is a significant legend. Living a life of prayer demands that we recognize our inner 'lion', the God-given flesh and its passions, not to be discarded (were that possible), but tamed and befriended.

St Jerome is not important so much as hermit, a rare blessedness for humanity, but as man-of-prayer, the common calling of us all, hermits and non-hermits alike. His prayer is based upon a sense of need, symbolized by his solitude, his nakedness, his agonized sorrow over sin. 'Sin' is a concept that only God can fully understand. All we know for certain is that we fail to receive his love in its fullness. He would give his peace to the world, but in us the gift is blocked.

The sacrament of penance is explicitly offered so that we may be purified in God's love and make it more present. Jerome is showing us here that prayer, to be real, must rise from the desire to love and be loved, to become vessels of the Holy Spirit for the suffering world about us.

Crivelli

St Peter, 1476

The power of scripture

St Peter looks cramped and confined here, partly because this is only half of Crivelli's St Peter and St Paul. But even with this excuse, the saint is still exceedingly compressed, squeezed coffin-like into a tall but narrow format, as if so much energy demands concentrated intensity.

The picture bristles with vitality, every section, however small, electric and alive. St Peter's surplice sweeps to the ground in tight dense folds, his outer vestment richly gilded and superbly embroidered, his great buckle gleaming, his tiara thick with jewelled ornament.

He is completely covered, even his hands smoothly shielded from the naked gaze: only his face is vulnerable. It is a memorable face, old and lived-in, with a massive hook of a nose and a densely lined forehead. The brooding eyes and the mouth, resolute and shut, are all the evidence Crivelli provides as to his subject's sanctity.

His St Peter is a man of complex activity. Both hands are fully occupied with the symbols of his holy office, the papacy, but it is the book we notice first, not the keys. This is a pope who grasps the stuff of command firmly enough, but whose rule is dependent upon the Book. The pictorial inserts on his garments show, probably, his brethren of the apostolic college, and each of these apostles too is cherishing the Book.

We feel that Peter is a burdened man, perhaps temperamentally a defensive man, silently sheltering within his massive officialdom. But he lives at peace with his burdens because, in the long run, they are not truly 'his': they are God's.

Without the Scriptures there is no knowledge of Jesus. What we read there opens up within us, revealing the truth of his reality. The sacred Scriptures are not primarily of intellectual value, though they are that too of course. They feed the mind with the Holiness of God, and from that holiness comes a life of union with him.

When we pray, it is Scripture that quietens us, that urges us to wait on the Lord, still and hopeful. This terse and elderly man, worried, decidedly tense, is yet a saint, not because he is a pope and an Apostle but because he cherishes the Word of God. However inhibiting his lifestyle (as suggested by the shape of the panel) the Book, the Holy Spirit made accessible to the longing heart, strengthens him to endure and to 'press forward'.

Crivelli shows us a saint under pressure, and all the more a saint because of it. Peter accepts his vocation and grapples with its demands: the help he needs is there, given by God, just as it is for us.

36

Veronese

The Consecration of St Nicholas, 1561-2

The people's choice

In medieval times, St Nicholas was frequently portrayed in art, mainly because his story contained so many delightful incidents. He is 'Santa Claus', the original Father Christmas, an Asian bishop who edified the midwives at his birth and kept up the pace throughout his life, and indeed after it, being posthumously credited with miraculous appearances at shipwrecks.

But giving balls of gold to destitute daughters (a dowry to save them from prostitution) or resuscitating small boys cannibalistically pickled in times of famine, had little visual appeal for the more sophisticated Renaissance artist. Veronese remembers St Nicholas, and remembers him with the utmost verve and chromatic glory, but the story he depicts is almost ordinary in comparison with what was theoretically on offer.

Nicholas, like other ancient bishops, was elected to his ecclesiastical office by popular acclaim. It was the people and the local clergy who seized upon him, yet a layman, and insisted that God had chosen him as their 'bishop'. (Although not present practice, this method of election seems at least as successful as the system we enjoy today!)

Veronese imagines the scene of consecration, clergy and people forming a ring around the reluctant saint. He is being almost forcibly invested in his surplice, still pleading for release from the burdens of this weighty responsibility.

But it is not just a popular choice: from above, God is ratifying it, and a glorious angel swoops down with the required episcopal vestments. The long diagonal of the crozier he bears angles down at the kneeling, beseeching saint while opposed to him, tall and upright, rears the processional cross, the sign of the Christian victory over death and grief. It is the cross that blocks Nicholas from refusal: his fear of an honour that is so demanding a responsibility must be countered by faith in Our Lord who empowers what is not humanly possible.

It is the uncontrollability of life that the painting stresses, the frightening truth of our helplessness to direct our own course. Nicholas does not want the priestly life: it is being chosen for him. The world outside the open window, green and lovely, is to be exchanged for the enclosed dimensions of a vocation to sacrificial service. But it is God who asks, and it is God Who will 'do it'.

He does not answer our prayers by changing circumstances: despite his entreaties Nicholas is still going to become a bishop. What God does do, and always will, is to make these circumstances fruitful and blessed: to make the most reluctant of us a saint.

Bernado Strozzi

St Catherine of Alexandria, c.1615-20

Betrothed to Christ

St Catherine is one of the great intellectual saints, and Strozzi has gone overboard to include every element of her legend.

She wears a crown, since she was held to be of royal descent, and her awesome learning is indicated by the books at and under her feet. In one hand she holds the wheel on which she was bound for martyrdom. It broke, miraculously, which is perhaps why she holds it so delicately, almost playfully. The emperor then had her beheaded, and so her other hand bears aloft the sword of her death and the palm of eternal life.

The most famous incident in her story was of her betrothal to Christ; he was said to have given her a ring, and this mystical marriage was the reason why Catherine could not accept any of the worldly suitors. The elaborate bracelet on her left arm, with its eyecatching ribbons, is intended to draw our attention to the ring which she unobtrusively wears on her finger. It is the least obvious of her attributes, but it is the most important. It was this betrothal to Christ, that was central to her story, that gave her a significance greater than that of any other saint except St Mary Magdalen.

In a sense, she was the church's contemporary replay of the Magdalen mystery, of a woman's complete surrender to Jesus, of her total love for him. 'They have taken away my Lord': Mary Magdalen is always portrayed as a passionate lover. But she is a 'sacred personage', one of the gospel characters. It would be easy to write off her intimacy with Jesus as peculiar to being contemporary with him.

Faith knows that this is not so, that Our Lord has transcended time and space by his Resurrection, and that we now live in him as completely as we desire. There are no obstacles except those of lack of intent. Holiness cannot be conditional on events or on people; it depends wholly and solely on whether we want God enough to take the trouble. Life spells out to us what he is asking, or more exactly, what he is giving.

For Catherine, it was a life of scholarship ended by martyrdom, but her lovely grave face looks out on us as if to impress the deeper truth, that God comes equally in any vocation. It was not the brilliance of her intellect, far less her birth and beauty that made her a saint: it was that she said 'yes' when Christ invited her to love him.

Jacopo Tintoretto

St George and the Dragon, 1560-80

The constant battle

Tintoretto died on 30 May, 400 years ago, though no artist has ever more radiantly exemplified the catechism statement that 'my soul can never die'. For all the rich Venetian gleam of his colour, it is the soul that Tintoretto paints, in the sense that our soul, our spirit, is the vital principle of our being, and that God himself is absolute Life.

No painter has ever made sheer divine energy as visible as Tintoretto, though unfortunately, (or fortunately, depending on whether you live in Italy or England), most of his greatest works are still in Venice, in the churches and palaces for which they were painted.

Still we have, in the National Gallery, his highly individual understanding of St George and the Dragon, unique, above all, in that our attention is focused, not on the hero battling (as the title suggests), but on the heroine enduring.

Tintoretto fills the foreground with the ample and distressed beauty of the captive princess. She seems just now to have fallen to her knees – energy held motionless – and she does not look behind her at the mortal combat. She is the one true solidity in the work. All behind her, a vast stretch of sea and coastland and the warrior on his gristly battlefield, seem strangely insubstantial.

It is in keeping with the way Tintoretto thinks visually that he may actually be suggesting that the setting is indeed insubstantial, that the real combat is in the mind of the praying woman. We all know, after all, that the dragon is not literally real, that it is a symbol for all that is dark within us, anti-love. St George too, is not historical, but equally a genuine symbol, the figure of the Saviour, a stand-in for Our Lord. Jesus and Sin, the total 'Yes' to the Father and the wild wish to say 'No': these battle it out in every heart at every moment.

But the moment of essential conflict, where the battle can become deadly, is in prayer. It is when we turn back on the actual battle, however emotionally aware of it we still are, and stretch out our praying hands to God, that we receive his deliverance.

Tintoretto depicts this, the act of prayer that is the passion of prayer, most subtly and strongly. Prayer is the most active passivity, the most passive activity: it is all surrender, receptivity, response. It is the only way to allow Jesus to rescue us from the great dragon of our selfishness.

Giovanni Bellini

The Assassination of St Peter Martyr, c.1507

Death preferred to resistance

Bellini's is a curious picture: in the background labourers are peacefully going about their daily affairs, while in the foreground two Dominican friars are being savagely hacked to death.

Perhaps it is significant that the workmen are cutting down trees, swinging the axe innocently while the assassins do so in malice. St Peter Martyr is shown in art with an axe embedded in his head, and the terrible violence of his death is emphasized by his very name, not just St Peter, but with Martyr added as a sort of honorific surname.

He was in fact one of the earlier Inquisitors, a profession that the modern conscience finds despicable. Without enquiring too exactly as to how Bellini would have seen it, this murder is shown to us as something cruel and brutal. The priests are unarmed, their attackers bristle with weapons.

The priests are defenceless in their white and black habits, the attackers massively armoured. One priest tries hopelessly to flee, while St Peter Martyr seemingly accepts the blows and surrenders himself to death. It was an event that shocked the contemporary Italian world and it retains its shock value. It is the shock of recognition, not the recognition that these things still happen, as they sadly do, but that we all have within us the potential to destroy what we find a threat. Self-defence is instinctive, and the assassins felt attacked by St Peter Martyr's crusade against their attitudes.

The problem is a delicate one: when have we the right to defend ourselves and to what degree? To hurt is wrong, of itself, whenever it means that another's good has been subordinated to one's own. Killing is the extreme form of this selfishness, but it has infinite modulations. We might know that to kill an 'enemy' is evil, or even wound him or her: what about verbal wounds, social aggression, the sheer selfishness that regards my own convenience as overriding that of all others?

St Peter Martyr preferred to die rather than risk the unrestraint of angry resistance – that is one extreme. The assassins chose to slaughter rather than submit to censure – that is the other.

We all have the responsibility to make decisions here, to align ourselves on one side or the other. Jesus died saying: Father, forgive them – and he added the only possible excuse: they know not what they do. May his example help us to forgive and never ignore the rights of our brothers and sisters.

Bacchicca

Tobias and the Angel

Revelation through prayer

Raphael makes only one appearance in the Scriptures, in the book of Tobias, but the part he plays there is that of the angelic hero.

His name means 'God has healed', and throughout this long and fascinating story, (a biblical novel), the angel incognito guides, protects and finally heals both the young Tobias and his blind father, the old Tobias. The healings are both physical and spiritual: Tobias the father has his sight restored, and Tobias the son has his life preserved from demonic attack.

All who meet the angel and accept him are visibly blessed: marriage safeguarded, fortune restored, well-being secured. The episode of young Tobias and the mysterious fish has attracted countless artists: Bacchicca shows the end of the adventure, when Tobias has captured the fish, biblically described as so great that 'it all but swallowed his foot'.

The fish here is a modest creature, a source of mild interest to Tobias's dog, but the youth is clearly awed by his encounter and his guide's enlightened counsel. He falls to his knees, and we are shown the angel's multi-coloured wings, as though the boy recognized the sacred nature of his helper. But the biblical story keeps recognition until the very end, when Raphael reveals himself, as if to underscore that we will never 'see' the angel, he must be 'shown' to us by revelation.

What Bacchicca is trying to make clear of course, is that this revelation comes in prayer. Tobias is not even looking at Raphael: his eyes are cast down and he has doffed his feathered cap, intent upon the reverence of prayer. The angel does not speak to him, merely looks down with infinite tenderness. God's compassion is always at work, healing and rescuing us, not visibly but truly. It is a wild and unknown world that we journey through, like Tobias. At all times, we advance under the creative love of God, his eyes notably looking at us with the deepest affection but actively affecting us.

The more aware we are of his presence, the more we are alert to respond. Our bodies will die, but God's healing will remain, transforming our whole being. To be healed, to have Raphael as companion, is a state of mind, a synonym for prayer.

Giovanni di Paolo

St Catherine of Siena Dictating her Dialogues to Raymond of Capua, 15th century

All wisdom is from God

St Catherine of Siena was one of the wonders of the fourteenth century. She only lived 33 years, her longing to die at the same age as Our Lord being fulfilled, but in that short time she exerted an immense influence.

She is a curious contradiction: not a nun, but a Tertiary of the Dominicans, living in her own home. She was an influential writer who was illiterate, dictating all her letters and treatises, a stigmatic whose wounds were visible only to herself, though in death they became clear to all.

She was too unconventional to receive universal approval, too dedicated to take any notice of the contempt. Her great good fortune was to be protected and guided by the Dominican fathers. One of the fathers, the Blessed Raymond of Capua, later to become Master General, is here shown as her confessor and scribe.

Giovanni di Paolo shows clearly the true dimensions of what was happening. Unseen by any save St Catherine, Jesus is telling her what to say, and she is repeating his words for Raymond to copy down. Whether this is how it actually happened is another matter, but di Paolo has seized upon the essentials. Anything that moves others to love God, to live in peace with their neighbours, to do their duty cheerfully, (St Catherine's great task was to persuade the pope to leave France and go back to live in Rome), all such messages come from God.

We do not necessarily have to know that 'all wisdom is from above': we may genuinely feel we thought of these things on our own. But where there is wisdom, even at the lowly stage of common sense, there is the Holy Wisdom of the Holy Spirit. A saint lives in this understanding of the mind of God, revealed to us through his Son, Jesus.

Hence the absolute need to read the Scriptures, slowly and prayerfully: there we find this wisdom in print for us. But these sacred Scriptures are difficult to understand. St Paul acknowledged this, and their true meaning unfolds only under the warmth of prayer.

St Catherine is shown on her knees, hands folded to indicate pure receptivity, eyes fixed, not on herself, but, in humility, on Jesus. The little room is bright with the revelation of divine love, but Jesus can only reveal his wisdom when there are 'ears to hear'. Our folly, selfish and greedy, stops the ears of the heart. May a humble intellectual, like St Catherine, help us to become open.

Sano di Petro

Stories from Life of St Blaise

The acceptance of human limitations

St Blaise was a martyr bishop from the early Christian era, around whom many legends gathered. He was said to have healed a small boy dying from a fish-bone stuck in his throat, hence the special blessing for the throat still given on his feastday.

This picture tells another favourite story, dear to the medieval heart. St Blaise was apparently a born vet, famous for healing all animals, wild and tame, and receiving their affectionate gratitude. When a poor woman wept to him that a wolf had carried off her pig, St Blaise simply asked his friend, the wolf, to return it.

St Blaise in full canonicals (just the thing for a stroll in the country) is blessing the woman at the left, while on the right, full foreground, the abashed wrongdoer makes restitution, the piglet still intact even to its curly tail.

Such a painting may seem childish to us, almost touching in its credulity, but Sano is delicately making some theological points. The saint, who is actually being arrested by the pagans in this episode (they lurk uneasily behind him), lives in an unprotected world: his background is deserted nature.

The woman, on the other hand, is a city-dweller, enclosed by massive and defensive walls. Sano is not contrasting the town and country, but suggesting why St Blaise can control the animal while the woman cannot.

He is in touch with his own animal-truth, he lives reverencing it. Because he respects the truth of his own body, he can see the truth of other animal bodies, and can heal and love them. No animal finds him a threat because he does not ever subordinate their good needlessly to his own. The key word is 'needlessly'. The woman is probably planning to kill and eat her pig one day, but it will be for its food value. Until she needs to, she must care for it.

Humankind has always harked back wistfully to the days, when, in Paradise, Adam and Eve were at home with the beasts, all God's creatures, all deserving of admiration. To be at ease with the animals is a token of ease with the ego, accepting human limitations and working with God within these limits.

How much pain and guilt and frustration have been caused by our desire to be as angels? Angels are immune to all our earthly weaknesses; without appetites, without needs, without emotions (or so we think). But God made us to have all these things, and to receive his love precisely in these humiliating conditions. St Blaise talking sweetly to the wolf is a man who understands his manhood.

Giovanni Battista Tiepolo

The Martyrdom of St Agatha, c.1750

Supreme faith of a martyr

Tiepolo the elder, though considered a great artist, is mainly admired as a supreme decorator. Yet no one has painted the meaning of faith, and its climax of martyrdom, more movingly than he.

The martyrdom of St Agatha is a picture almost unbearable in its intensity of love. Her story is a particularly gory one, even for the early legends, and it included one torture that stuck in the Christian consciousness: she had her breasts cut off. Artists have usually depicted this with repulsive literalness: the saint is accompanied by a plate on which rest two blancmange-shaped mounds. Those indelicate mounds are here, too, but so subtly and tactfully that we almost miss them. Tiepolo's attention is not on the body but on the spirit.

Agatha knows she is dying, in great pain, and drained of blood. She is overshadowed by the threatening bulk of her executioner, and her supporters are distraught and youthful. We are given a picture that is confused, noisy, hopeless.

Agatha ignores her surroundings. With unshaken confidence she looks heavenward, even as her eyes glaze over from agony and loss of blood. With her last strength she raises her hands to her God, not so much imploring as gesturing for his attention. She silently shows herself to him, and waits.

This is the very essence of prayer. It is not we who address God, but he who addresses us. Prayer exposes to him what we are, all our mutilations, our pains, our weakness. God always sees our heart, seeing there what we have not yet seen ourselves: he alone truly knows us, and whatever our self-love, God's love is greater.

Nothing can put him off, no sin, no malice. He loves us with total affection. But in prayer we surrender to this love. We actively open ourselves and allow him, desire him, to flood us with his presence.

We do not need to articulate any request: Agatha says nothing, merely acts. In offering her being she is expressing her trust, not in temporal rescue, but in eternal redemption. She knows in whom she has believed, and that he is tenderly aware of what is being done to her. She goes down into a dreadful death looking steadfast at Jesus, her Redeemer. This is, of all great works of art, one that is wholly unforgettable.

Perugino

St Lucy, 1505

Total yearning for God

It was rumoured in Renaissance Florence that Perugino was an atheist, but it is difficult to believe this: his saints are so serene, blissfully intent on heaven. There is an upward gaze, solemn and direct, that often characterized his images, though in this case the emphasis on the eyes is probably the result of the legend about St Lucy.

Early on, her name suggested a connection with light, and so with sight, and she was thought to have had her eyes put out in her martyrdom. Visually she usually bears resemblance to a hideous stalk with eyes on either end, or else a dish with eyeballs in it.

Perugino, sophisticate that he is, scorns such literalness. His St Lucy holds a cup of fire, delicately positioned near her heart, parted tongues of flame that suggest the Holy Spirit at Pentecost. Her other hand holds a book, since love and knowledge go together.

If we do not know God, how can we love him? And if we do not love him, what use is our knowledge? Ignorant love is, of its nature, false. Love craves to know, to understand, to enter into the mood of the beloved. With God, the process is almost terrible in its simplicity. We know the Lord through using our minds: reading, meditating, asking questions.

But we know him also from our hearts: praying, surrendering, keeping silence. One attitude complements the other: they are both indispensable. But we only take the time and trouble to do all this if we earnestly desire it. Wanting God is the essential prerequisite, and that is the central theme of Perugino's picture.

St Lucy holds the book of knowledge and the chalice of love but all her attention is on what is above. Her look is one of profound yearning. We are convinced that she 'sees', not in any literal sense, but mystically. Balaam in the Old Testament has a revelation which he describes as: 'I see him, but not in the present; I behold him but not near at hand.'

It is that distant seeing which strengthens St Lucy to say a total Yes to the Father. She wants, with all that is in her, for God to take possession of her being. That undeviating choice is what holiness is all about: from it flow all the acts of love and wisdom. St Lucy, woman of light, looks with desire into the mystery of God.

El Greco

St Bernardine of Siena

The power of the holy name

By all accounts, St Bernardine was a man of great austerity, and El Greco is a perfect painter for him. But it is not because of his specific life-story that El Greco portrays the saint as long and thin: for El Greco, anyone who aspired to God was spiritually elongated, whatever their actual form.

His St Bernardine shoots upwards like a slender arrow, totally vertical. He stands amidst minor vertical ties, the mitres that he scorned and, far in the distance, the protective city towers that he left behind in his wandering apostolate.

He holds the book, but holds it vertically, his slender form is bisected by the long Franciscan cord, binding him to God by the three vows, indicated by the three knots.

His travelling staff is as thin and tall almost as the saint himself, but he uses it to proclaim his greatest devotion, to the Holy Name of Jesus: IHS. There may be a secret reference to Constantine's banner: *In Hoc Signo (vinces)*.

Certainly St Bernardine believed that 'in this sign' we would conquer, the sign being a loving and slow uttering of the Holy Name. It was decried as superstitious, even in his own days, though in the end Rome upheld his othodoxy, but his preaching makes fine psychological sense. All our acts of self-love, all our sins, come from a forgetting of Jesus.

We cannot think of him, truly, and then wantonly cast his love away. We plunge into wrong before we are aware: thinking of the Holy Name holds us back long enough for sanity to take over. But it is not just a therapeutic measure.

There is power in the very Name, something all pagan religions know. To know someone's name means to have power over them, however external: they will, after all, turn round for you if you name them aloud, stop in their tracks, look up.

Only God knows our full true name, that creative name that will make us be what we are capable of being. In prayer, we come closer and closer to becoming able to hear it, and in death, it will sound out for us.

Jesus has freely given us his name, which means 'Saviour'. It has extraordinary power: do we use it?

Jan van Eyck

St Barbara

Contemplation is not deprivation

Jan van Eyck's drawing of St Barbara is famous not only for its extraordinary beauty but for its value as social history.

He shows the saint sitting before her emblem, a tower, but this is a tower in the course of construction, and every detail of the building process in the background is of importance to historians.

There we see a world of disciplined activity, labourers all hard at work on the building site while various conditions of men press into the completed portions: foremen? worshippers? There is a cross above the main portal which suggests that this is a church tower. The legend of St Barbara described her as having been immured in a tower by her pagan father, and it has always been her emblem. Here she sits elegantly before it, a real tower in a real world, with small field and hills to the right and a distant town looming on the left. Barbara is uninterested: she is in the world, that active, teeming and fascinating world, but she pays it no attention. Even the palm of her martyrdom (inflicted by her father, who beheaded her and was then struck by lightning, causing St Barbara to be elected as the patron saint of the artillery) is held with unconcern.

What holds Barbara's attention is her book. With his wonderful clarity of detail, van Eyck makes it obvious to us this is a breviary or Book of Hours. The saint is looking at an illuminated page, gazing, not merely reading: she is using the book as a means of prayer. Her body language speaks of restful attentiveness.

Her very garments are so convincing in their amplitude, her skirt spreading around her like a small mountain, too long for her to be able to walk in it, too thick in its stately folds for her to be able to carry the weight of it.

It is a symbolic skirt, like the great expanse of sleeve above: nobody could work manually with such a sleeve, hence its cultural status in the fifteenth century. The belt too, and the tiny waist it encircles, are both fashionable and symbolic: Barbara has all the luxuries of the world, but she scorns them. She chooses contemplation, as evidenced by the enclosure of her impractical dress: within the dimensions of this cloth, back turned to the life of action, she will muse on the things of God.

Van Eyck does not show the contemplative life as a deprived one, but rather as enormously rich and happy. Little St Barbara sits alone and deeply content.

Francisco de Zurbarán

St Apollonia

Death is also new life

St Apollonia was actually an aged deaconess, whose martyrdom included having all her teeth knocked out, but Zurbarán invariably painted his women saints as young, beautiful and extremely fashionable.

This, he seems to say, is the real saint, this gracious and charming lady, dressed to the nines and yet moving purposefully towards a terrible death at the call of fidelity.

St Apollonia holds her martyr's palm with casual disdain, barely touching it. It rests against the amplitude of her costly skirt like a long and decorative feather. Her special attribute, a pair of dental pincers holding a tooth – matter for nightmare – is gripped firmly enough, but pointed away from her.

Her neat little mouth gives no indication that she is toothless, and though she accepted the instrument of her torment she does not brandish it with any personal interest. What Zurbarán depicts is a saint's interest in the end, never in the means.

St Apollonia is dressed as for a celebration, her curls adorned with well-ordered roses, her lovely mantle fastened with an elaborate bow and brooch, every element of her costume elegant in its costly simplicity. She looks out at us with a serious tranquillity, a young woman prepared for her vocation. This vocation will entail pain, and end in a humiliating death: she accepts this, sadly but not tragically. What matters to her is where this pain will take her, and she knows that it can only be to her Lord. Nothing in life has meaning of itself. Obviously, we would not all choose to have our teeth knocked out, but if that dread event should befall us, then the only concern is how to use it, how not to waste it, how to turn it into good.

God does not intervene to change the circumstances of our life: what he does do, with the most compassionate faithfulness, is enable us to make those circumstances fruitful. Death remains death but it is also new life: pain accepted from his hands purifies, transforms, redeems.

A martyrdom is a celebration if we allow God to use it in and for us. God is what happens to us, his presence makes everything potential for growth in love and goodness.

St Apollonia, small and sweet, all dressed up for death because she believes in her Lord, is a symbolic expression of this.

.S.POLO
NIA.

Orazio Borgianni

St Charles Borromeo, c.1610-16

Healing by grace

Borgianni is a minor artist, and St Charles Borromeo is not one of the well-known saints, yet this is a striking image of what it means to love God totally.

St Charles has accepted a cardinal's hat, but it lies behind a skull, recalling not the honour of the cardinalate but its responsibilities: we have only a short time in the world and must not waste it. (St Charles died in his mid-40's, exhausted from his work during the plague.)

The red hat is also flanked by two books, since no understanding of God is real if we do not use the means we have at hand; and spiritual reading is one of them. But it must not be arid reading, feeding the mind alone, and so a crucifix is laid across the book. The great significance of the Cross is not that it urges us to mortification, but that it makes clear that life – and death – are full of suffering; there is no easy way to live or die.

Pain, like joy, can be turned selfishly inwards and tie us up with ego-concern. It is meant to teach us trust, to open our heart to the reality of God, to be redemptive, as it was for Our Lord. The grace to turn bitterness into sweetness and let suffering make us holy comes from prayer and the sacraments, and so the altar stands next to St Charles. At worship, his prayer will be taken up into the prayer of Jesus and energize his day. For now, Borgianni shows him preparing for worship, not yet fully vested. It is a baroque painting, highly emotional, but none the less a moving record of genuine faith.

St Charles does not seem to be using words: he simply looks up to God with complete conviction, offering himself to be healed by grace. This saint knew intimately what grace could achieve, since he had a far from easy struggle towards goodness. He was the pope's nephew; a typical example of Renaissance abuse of clerical power made him an abbot at twelve and he was a cardinal before he was ordained priest.

He was considered mentally slow, and he stuttered, a dull delicate youth. Yet he fought tenaciously to become a good and educated priest, and then, when he finally received pastoral office, to be a good bishop to Milan.

He fought almost alone, his clergy on one occasion trying to assassinate him. But his desire to follow Our Lord drew him to a completely selfless life of prayer and pastoral work. Something of this intensity of direction comes across in this painting. His bony hands are tense with longing for his God, and his plain and peaceful countenance is alight with love from him.

Here is one who let God make him holy.

Part Two

Images of Love

detail of a page from Genesis in Hebrew, Provence, probably Avignon, c.1422

Inadequate images of the creator

The Jewish fear of making 'a graven image' has a certain wisdom when it is applied directly to the Godhead.

The Christian Bible might well illuminate *Initio* – in the beginning – but it would be likely to follow the word with an illustration of that sacred beginning. We would see the Creator in his majesty, shaping heaven and earth out of nothingness, or calling into being animate life.

The supreme example of this is the Sistine chapel ceiling, and yet, even there, how far short it must fall! The poetry of our beginning is a secret known to God alone. Even when we solve the facts of it, which is not impossible, the real meaning of those facts, their truth, will never be comprehensible by a finite intelligence. So there is a lovely appropriateness in the abstraction of the Hebrew. Even the letters for 'in the beginning', for those of us ignorant of the Hebrew alphabet, appear as abstraction, and the artist has reinforced this by the background decoration and the surrounding diamond pattern.

The choice of the diamond form is apt: our making is a thing of wonder, of brilliance and brightness, and the golden gleam of the pattern suggests this sublimal glory. It is diamond hard, too: an absolute for God.

He once and for all extended the sphere of his divinity – to use crude human terms – and created creatures who were from now and for ever partakers, darkly yet integrally, in that mysterious Life. The great majesty of the lettering speaks of the majesty of our origin.

We began in radiance and spaciousness, infinitely privileged. God must always have known that the majority of his children would never be aware, consciously, of their birth from the touch of his shaping Hand.

His vegetable and animal children, his atmospheric children – the winds, the heats, the planets, the stars – none of these definitions, (or so it seems to us) can respond to him willingly and with full intelligence. It is only we who are called to give a voice to the wordless prayer of creation, and we can only do that in confidence because we have Jesus, the Son as opposed to the Child, the One who looks at the Holy mystery and tells us how to respond. And of those who are blessed to believe in Jesus, how few there are!

The blessing carries the great weight of responsibility in that we have to receive the light of Jesus, repeat knowingly the words of Jesus, open our hearts to the power of the Spirit of Jesus, not just for inanimate or non-human creation, but for our fellow humans who 'know not what they do'.

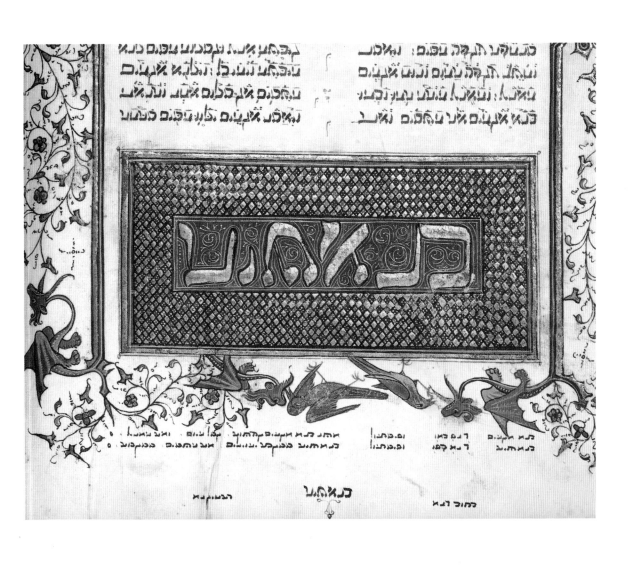

Caravaggio

The Taking of Christ

Hands of love and hate

The taking of Christ is a violent picture. Caravaggio, himself a man of violence (and in the end destroyed by it), depicts every actor in this scene as emotionally distraught – all except for Jesus.

The disciples flee in open-mouthed terror, the soldiers surge forward angrily intent on seizure, Judas grasps his Lord grimly and terribly, intent upon betrayal.

Only Jesus stays quiet, surrendering himself to his passion. We are shown distorted faces and bewildered faces: the soldiers clearly do not fully grasp what they are doing: 'Befehl ist befehl!' But the sad face of the central figure, pushed to one side, as is the manner of betrayal but inherently central, is remote in silent prayer. Jesus grieves, not only for himself, but for the friend who has sacrificed his own wholeness in sacrificing Jesus. Caravaggio tells the story partly through faces but even more through hands. The highest point in the painting is an aggressive hand, and a hand raised in blind fear comes just below, which is of significance.

In the middle area are the hand of Judas, digging fiercely into Jesus' arm, and the overlaid hand, non-human in its steel protection, of the arresting officer. This man dominates the foreground, almost faceless, like a huge beetle, destroying what it catches. But right at the bottom, strongly lit, are the linked hands of Jesus, resolute in non-resistance, tense but peaceful, hands braced to receive what the Father allows to happen. It is this painful but total obedience that is most integral to the meaning of Jesus. His eyes are not set on any outward happening, only on the presence within of the silent Spirit.

Caravaggio shows him, not as consoled or indifferent. No, he is a 'man like we are, knowing weakness'. But he can cling in his weakness and sorrow to his Father, cling with an absolute sureness, whatever he may feel or endure. 'Though he slay me, yet will I trust in him.'

The turmoil of life is not something to be escaped, but to be used. Caught in the net of malice (symbolized by the flying cloak that wraps Jesus and Judas together), Jesus waits in patience for his deliverance, not from disaster but through it. In him, we too are free when entrapped, empowered to make all our distress a holy purification.

Only a willing surrender to love can truly 'take' us, and those who come to 'take' are unwitting instruments of that love. Judas 'takes' Jesus to the death that will be his own redemption as well as ours.

Michael Finn

Flying Crucifix, 1990

Set free to soar to heaven

If we have ever seen hang-gliders, we know that the human body can, with help, experience the wonders of flight. By instinct we know the stance, with arms held wide in imitation of a bird's wings, with head held high, looking hopefully upwards, with feet on tiptoe, ready for the soaring.

Without the elaborate apparatus of the hang-glider, we remain solidly earthbound, however, and it is on this constant human longing, to be and do what is not of our nature, that Michael Finn is playing in 'Flying Crucifix'.

It is a small work, about 25 inches high, all rough wood roughly painted. Jesus spreads his arms, and soars. The cross becomes visible to us, not as what nails him down, grounds him, but as the instrument of his flight into holy freedom. Before the cross, Jesus endured the constraints of the earth. Now, having given up to the uttermost his own will ('Not my will, but thine be done'), he is enabled to go where nature cannot take him.

Suffering and death are never intended as destructions, as obstacles to fullness of being. They become so, all too often, because we refuse to give up our will and to seek in the pain the divine meaning. Jesus trusted his father too absolutely not to hold in faith that the agony was life-giving.

He experienced, Scripture suggests, unrelieved anguish, including the astonishing sense (almost beyond our imagination) that he had been 'forsaken'. Yet Jesus clung in faith to the certainty that this was how it *felt*. It could not be how it *was* because the father can never forsake those who love him.

Relying then on nothing human, on no feeling or consolation, exposed to the naked truth of faith, Jesus is set free to soar into total joy. Finn shows this by painting the cross itself a delicate blue. It is the blue of the skies, the colour of that heaven where Jesus lives, where he most truly already is, while at the same time – *because* at the same time – he hangs upon the scaffold.

We do not see any details of the face of Jesus. He has already flown beyond recognition in this detailed sense. He is most radiantly himself, broad-chested and austere: blood and pain, nails and cross, have all been transformed into the glory of ascension.

Jenny Franklin

Winged Earth, 1991

The acceptance of truth

At first sight, *Winged Earth* both seems and sounds a paradox. Isn't earth precisely that which does not fly, which lies beneath, which is wingless? And doesn't the work itself give us a sense of vertigo, as if wheeling down from a great height? We see the wings, ruffled angel feathers, but attached to what?

The great central shape is too exact, too neatly tooled to be mere landscape. It ends on the lower right in a curve of parrot-beak, and it cut to the left by the geometrical violence of a triangle.

We have a true sense of wingedness, of great altitude, and a clear sense of earth, that quilt of field and mountain. But how do the two unite? Perhaps the answer is they do not literally.

At one level, art must always deal with the real visible world, not to repeat its visibility but to make visible what only art can achieve. Only the artist can take us to an earth that has wings, where we can fly and be on the ground simultaneously.

Franklin, one of our great contemporary colourists, does this through the intensity and purity of her vision. We are drawn away from our narrow certainties into the lovely expanses of the artist's world.

There is no space here for the littleness of the ego, for the imprisoning anxieties of a self-centred life. There is no pretence at escape. Franklin accepts a sun without lustre, a ruptured earth, a sinister cloudiness at the centre. But she transcends it all by the radiant affirmation of those opinions.

Whatever the conditions, we were created for flight, for freedom, for joy. We shall get there by accepting what is and seeking its inner truth.

What we see may not be at all what essentially is. Truth in itself may 'hurt', and so we avoid it. But in the accepting comes the awareness of the beyond, the wingedness of the soil.

Look well, the artist hints. But Franklin is the most subtle and delicate of hinters. The 'meaning' is in the work, not outside it, not capable of being extracted and put into words. All the more reason then, to look well. It is only in the looking, the act of contemplation, that we become free to understand.

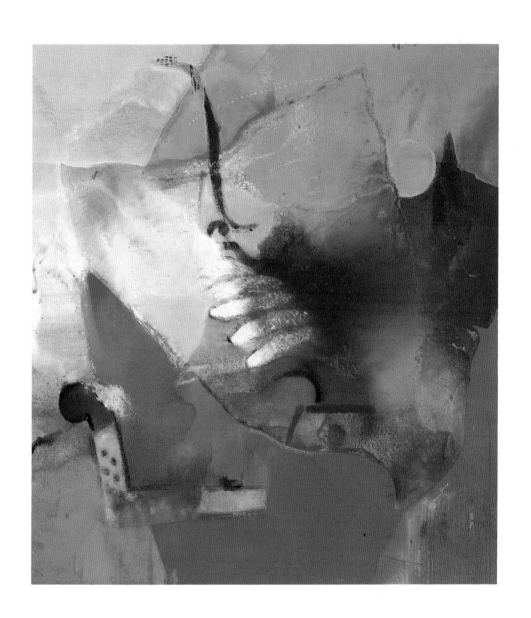

Simon Lewty

Pointing Man, 1990

The word of God in graffiti

Simon Lewty is best known as a map-maker, fabulous maps to places of the spirit. Yet he convinces us that they are real places, if only we had the courage to venture out into the non-material world.

Maps, which are in themselves both text and picture, have a deep fascination for him. Inscription is part of his artistic practice, not in the sense of writing intelligibly but more in the sense of the graffiti artists.

His imagination is held by the images long-dead and forgotten people have scribbled upon stone, now revealed to us, their posterity, in all their mysteriousness.

There is a sense that what intrigues Lewty is the illegibility of what is written, the essential impossibility of truly communicating with one another.

We are all locked up in our own solitude, he seems to brood, and the most we can do is 'point'. 'Pointing man' is clearly suffering. Is he running past the stone walls or do they hem him in? Everything about this pointing figure seems tense with motion, with the effort of running, yet he has only one shoe and is ill-equipped, in his skin-tight costume, for the race.

But his costume too has graffiti over it, as though this really were skin and he was tattooed with other men's inscriptions. Even more, some of the writing goes over him onto the vellum-like page, as if he were actually imprisoned on it.

No wonder this poor man screams in soundless distress and has been abruptly truncated at the top of his head, his reasoning power. He lives in a world he cannot understand or escape from: lonely, frightened, tense. At what is he pointing? He seems not to know; his eyes look both ways, and his head stares directly out at the viewer. In one way this presents a terrifying image of what it must be like to be genuinely alone. This, of course, is something the Christian believer can never be: 'I am not alone, the Father is with me.'

In a very profound way, it is only when we accept to be 'alone' – vulnerable, unsupported by public opinion, living by your own principles and accepting their consequences, that we can realize the non-aloneness of the Christian.

While we are muffling the truth with noise and conformities, Jesus cannot take us into the companionship that he gives in prayer to those who desire him. We have to understand, look without pretence at the meaningless of what our senses perceive – and then God can give everything true meaning in himself. Then graffiti turns into writing, the word of God.

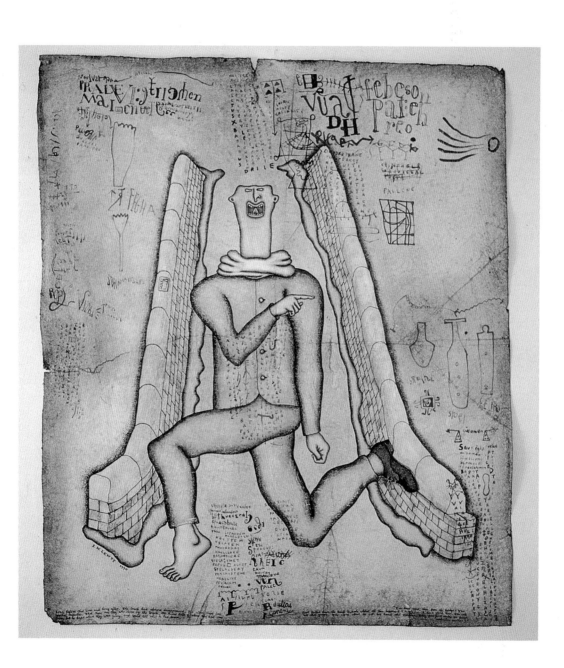

Robert Mason

The Bowl (of Emotions), 1984

Disclosure equals an act of prayer

Robert Mason's whole family – father, mother, brother, sister – were found to be suffering from a slowly degenerative disease. His father, the last to die, left him a bitter and despairing letter. Trying to come to terms with his loneliness, grief and anger, seeking to exorcise them in this art, to find some meaning in impersonal values: this preoccupied Mason until, nearing 40, he has been able to succeed. His early work was cathartic.

Now, even if perilously so, he has freed himself from vain resentments and can use his sorrow creatively and truly. It colours all he does, as a haunting awareness of man's mortality, but this gives an added human dimension. He no longer flees, he accepts and makes his peace, and in so doing, finds his centre.

The title *Disclosure* fits all his recent work, in that he is seeking to unveil – not his own privacy, but the heart of man. Such disclosure is always fragmentary, veiled in its very attempt at unveiling, and so his naked man, bending to the bowl, is half hidden in mists and looming brightness. Is it a bowl in which the emotions are purified? Is he washing himself free of emotions or in his emotions?

The latter, probably, since he is a deeply personal painter. At last, able to accept his emotions as pure, he can approach them with naked foot. But until we can acknowledge emotion – pour it into a bowl, have a towel at hand – it is a potentially disruptive force within. Maybe the incandescent swirls on the image express this symbolically, express it and resolve it, as we do in Jesus.

What Mason really depicts here is the act of prayer.

Paul Klee

The Order of the High C.1921

Aiming high

Klee was a great lover of music: his wife taught the piano, and he himself was a violinist of professional quality. He saw music – like art – as sacramental, a way of communion with God. But real communion is rooted in our own reality, our pathetic and almost humorous littleness. Of all Klee's countless music pictures, this is one of my favourites, both delightful and profound.

He imagines that those few singers who can reach High C should be given an 'order; – a decoration like the order of the garter; and so this little singer's head is shaped like a medallion, with presentation ribbons behind.

But it is only medal-shaped because she has put all that is in her into her high note. Her very mouth has become a 'c', her hair is formed from musical staves, and her throat has dwindled to nothing but a source of song.

In her intense concentration her desire to be wholly and purely that true high note, she doesn't see that she has drawn into herself all the brightness of the picture. When the faint background colours reach this dedicated head, they spring into light. She is almost a light bulb, radiating song.

And in another sense this is 'The Order of the High C', the religious order of those who wholly give themselves to the highest.

We are not High C, Jesus is. He forms himself on the lips of those who narrow and compress all their energies into becoming his music.

Funny little singer, but the more we look (and listen) the more we can be lost with her in the only thing that matters, the Jesus proof, the clear high note that he will sing within the self-forgetful heart.

Anthony Caro

Early One Morning, 1962

Acceptance, not expectation

Caro began as an assistant to Henry Moore, though it is difficult now to see any trace of the Master's powerful massiveness. Perhaps Caro has reacted, because his work is as slender and unsupported as Moore's is large.

Yet what delicate beauty in this inspired daring! *Early One Morning* attempts to express a mood, to create a purely abstract arrangement of branching steel that will compel us into an experience. Wild and free, gracious only by secret rules of its own making, it springs forth in its nakedness to challenge us.

To enter into its meaning, we must be completely without prejudice or predisposition. If we 'expect' the sculpture we traditionally love we shall be profoundly disconcerted. Only the free mind can respond to this wayward grace and demand nothing more than the sculptor modestly sets before us.

Our expectations and demands so frequently rob us of beauty. Our prayer is poor and naked, and we write it off. Our sisters are not what we would desire, so we never see the shy possibilities there. We would like a life of *our* fashioning.

Be still, says Caro, look at my lowly sculpture and respond to what I have made. How much more does Jesus say this, and how much beauty he has made all around us, early and late, every morning.

Michael Finn

Crucifix, 1985-6

Confronted by the form of the cross

This is a big crucifix, nearly five feet high, and the reproduction does not truly expose us to the encounter of the reality: the large and compelling presence, the physicality of sheer size, has to be experienced imaginatively.

What makes the encounter dramatic is the austerity of means that Michael Finn has used. Black cross, white figure, minimal moulding.

Although the figure of the Lord is shaped from gesso, that paintable plaster, Finn seems to have abjured the use of colour as somehow unbefitting. Jesus has sacrificed his everything, has surrendered to an absolute of denudation. The artist echoes and thus emphasizes this in his own chromatic starkess. Jesus is drained, bloodless for our sake. But the shed blood too is colourless.

All that is bright and makes any demands upon the eye has been expunged here: we are confronted solely with the kenosis of the Saviour. Nothing compels our attention by itself: it is our own choice that must move us to stand up and compassionate him, seeking to understand the meaning of this self-emptying. The holy body too is rendered without any attempt at naturalistic shaping.

The arms visibly slot uneasily into the body, the torso is a bare sketch of musculature, the stick-like legs are rigid. The face has merely enough feature to remain recognizable as human, yet how touching is its drawn and suffering lineaments.

Finn's Jesus is already dead, asleep in the Father but still pressed almost into nothingness by the weight of the agony. He makes no overt appeals to us, he is visibly concentrated upon his prayer, that innermost secret of the soul of Jesus that is the essence, still hidden and secret, even to us, of our own prayer.

The Finn Crucifix is a work of the most profound silence. In the stillness of his surrender, Jesus gives up all he is and could have been. Even emotion, even consciousness of what this sacrifice really is, is absent here. We are shown only the meaning of what faith puts before us, and we either offer our own hearts to receive the prayer of Jesus, or we refuse.

Before such a humble abandoned Jesus, the price of refusing – not to have part of him – is surely too terrible? He makes no demands: he will do it all, if only we accept him.

acknowledgements

DUCCIO *The Calling of the Apostles Peter and Andrew*, 1308/11. Samuel H Kress Collection. Photograph © 1995 Board of Trustees, National Gallery of Art, Washington

ROGIER VAN DER WEYDEN *Magdalen Reading*, c. 1435. Courtesy of the Trustees, The National Gallery, London

LORENZO LOTTO *Holy Family with St Anne*, 1535. Princes Gate Collection. Photograph © Courtauld Institute Galleries, London

LUCA GIORDANO *St Michael the Archangel*, c.1663. Gemäldegalerie, Staatliche Museen, Berlin. Photograph © Artothek

LORENZO LOTTO *St Catherine of Alexandria*, 1522. Samuel H Kress Collection. Photograph © 1995 Board of Trustees, National Gallery of Art, Washington

GIOTTO *St Francis Preaching to the Birds*. Musée du Louvre. Photograph © R.M.N.

RAPHAEL *St George and the Dragon*, c.1506. Andrew W Mellon Collection. Photograph © 1995 Board of Trustees, National Gallery of Art, Washington

GIROLAMO DA CREMONA detail from *Frontispiece: Aristotle "Opera"*, Vol II, Venice de Blavis and Torresanus, 1483. PML 21195, ChL ff907. The Pierpont Morgan Library, New Your, U.S.A. Photograph © The Pierpont Morgan Library, 1995

RAPHAEL *An Allegory (Vision of a Knight)*, c. 1504. Courtesy of the Trustees, The National Gallery, London

EUSTACHE LE SUEUR *The Annunciation*, c. 1650. The Toledo Museum of Art, Toledo, Ohio. Purchased with funds from the Libbey Endowment. Gift of Edward Drummond Libbey

BARTOLOME MURILLO *The Infant St John with a Lamb*, 1660/5. Courtesy of the Trustees, The National Gallery, London

GEORGES DE LA TOUR *St Sebastian and Irene*. Musée du Louvre. Photograph © R.M.N.

LORIN DE CHARTRES (studio of) Alsation School, *St Timothy with the Martyrs' Palm*, mid 12th century, removed from Neuwiller Abbey. Musée Cluny, Paris. Photograph © Giraudon/Bridgeman Art Library

DIEGO VELAZQUEZ *St John the Evangelist*, c. 1618 Courtesy of the Trustees, The National Gallery, London

ANDREA DEL SARTO *St Agnes*. Duomo, Pisa. Photograph © Scala

MICHELINO DA BESOZZO *St Luke Painting the Virgin*, from a Prayer Book, Italy, (Milan), c. 1420. M.944, f.75v. The Pierpont Morgan Library, New York, U.S.A. Photograph © The Pierpont Morgan Library/Art Resource, NY

GIOVANNI BATTISTA CIMA DA CONEGLIANO *St Jerome in a Landscape*, c. 1500/10. Courtesy of the Trustees, The National Gallery, London

CRIVELLI *St Peter* (from The Demidoff Altarpiece), 1476. Courtesy of the Trustees, The National Gallery, London

VERONESE *The Consecration of St Nicholas*, 1561/2. Courtesy of the Trustees, The National Gallery, London

BERNADO STROZZI *St Catherine of Alexandria*, c. 1615/20. Photograph courtesy of Wadsworth Atheneum. The Ella Gallup Sumner and Mary Catlin Sumner Collection Fund and Endowed by Mrs A Everett Austin, JR.

JACOPO TINTORETTO *St George and the Dragon*, 1560/80. Courtesy of the Trustees, The National Gallery, London

GIOVANNI BELLINI *The Assassination of St Peter Martyr*, c. 1507. Courtesy of the Trustees, The National Gallery, London

BACCHICCA *Tobias and the Angel*. Courtesy of Wadsworth Atheneum, Hartford. The Ella Gallup Sumner and Mary Catlin Sumner Collection Fund. Photograph © David Stansbury, 1993

GIOVANNI DI PAOLO *St Catherine of Siena Dictating Her Dialogues to Raymond of Capua*, 15th century. The Detroit Institute of Arts, 1995, Founders Society Purchase, Ralph Harman Booth Bequest Fund, Joseph H Boyer Memorial Fund, Building Endowment Fund, Mr and Mrs Benson Ford Fund, Henry Ford II

SANO DI PETRO *Stories from Life of St Blaise: The Wolf Returning the Pig to the Poor Widow*. Pinacoteca, Siena. Photograph © Edimedia

GIOVANNI BATTISTA TIEPOLO *The Martyrdom of St Agatha*, c.1750. Gemäldegalerie, Berlin. Photograph © Artothek

PERUGINO *St Lucy*, 1505. Photograph by Schecter Lee © 1996 The Metropolitan Museum of Art. Gift of The Jack and Belle Linsky Foundation, Inc.,1981. (1981.293.2)

EL GRECO *St Bernardine of Siena*. Museo del Greco, Toledo. Photograph © Scala

JAN VAN EYCK *St Barbara*. Koninklijk Museum voor Shone Kunsten, Plaatsnijdersstraat, Antwerp. Photograph © Scala

FRANCISCO DE ZURBARAN *St Apollonia*. Musée du Louvre, Paris. Photograph © R.M.N.

ORAZIO BORGIANNI *St Charles Borromeo*, c. 1610/16. Hermitage, St Petersburg. Photograph © Bridgeman Art Library

Detail of a page from GENESIS, bible written in Hebrew, Provence, probably Avignon, c. 1422. G.48, f.17v detail. The Pierpont Morgan Library, New York, U.S.A. Photograph © The Pierpont Morgan Library/Art Resource, NY

CARAVAGGIO *The Taking of Christ*. Courtesy of the National Gallery, Ireland

MICHAEL FINN *Flying Crucifix*, 1990. Photograph courtesy of John and Ella Halkes Collection

JENNY FRANKLIN *Winged Earth*, 1991. Photograph courtesy of Crane Kalman Gallery, London

SIMON LEWTY *Pointing Man*, 1990. Photograph courtesy of Art First, London

ROBERT MASON *The Bowl (of Emotions)*, 1984. Photograph courtesy of Anne Berthoud Gallery

PAUL KLEE *The Order of the High C*, 1921. Private Collection. Photograph © Estate of the Artist. © DACS 1996

ANTHONY CARO *Early One Morning*, 1962. Tate Gallery Collection. Photograph courtesy of the artist

MICHAEL FINN *Crucifix*, 1985/6. Courtesy of the artist